DOUBLE-HEADED TRAINS

Dave Smith

AMBERLEY

Front cover: Direct Rail Services' Class 20s Nos 20302 and 20304 head west at Grange-over-Sands, working 6C52, the Heysham–Sellafield nuclear flasks, on 15 July 2003.

Rear cover: Loadhaul-liveried Class 56 No. 56118 helps failed EWS No. 60035, working 6F45, the Tees Yard–Skinningrove steel empties, past Hunt Cliff on 10 September 2002.

First published 2018

Amberley Publishing
The Hill, Stroud
Gloucestershire, GL5 4EP

www.amberley-books.com

Copyright © Dave Smith, 2018

The right of Dave Smith to be identified as the Author of this work has been asserted in accordance with the Copyright, Designs and Patents Act 1988.

ISBN 978 1 4456 7364 6 (print)
ISBN 978 1 4456 7365 3 (ebook)

British Library Cataloguing in Publication Data.
A catalogue record for this book is available from the British Library.

Origination by Amberley Publishing.
Printed in the UK.

Introduction

As a well-travelled railway photographer, I was delighted to have been asked by Amberley to put together a colourful collection of railway double-headed trains.

With many changes in recent years since privatisation, double-headed trains have brought much added interest to the UK rail scene, with its many different companies, local types and liveries, making for interesting times ahead.

Since the original BR colours (pre-privatisation), many changes have occurred on the motive power front, with the introduction of new classes such as 66s, 68s and 70s in modern times.

Selecting photographs for this book was a difficult task, as I wanted to include the greatest variety in terms of locomotive, classes and traffic on different lines, while at the same time produce a selection of photographs that was interesting, scenic, and had an emphasis on the more exciting workings in the UK. I have also included triple- and quadruple-headed trains for added interest.

Having amassed many thousands of hours by the lineside, it is this enjoyable but sometimes frustrating hobby that has produced this pictorial collection, which presents a wide-ranging selection of modern-day images taken around the UK, dating from 1999 to the present day.

I would like to dedicate this book to my late Gramp, George Wilby, for introducing me to an interest that has become my hobby from the age of six. I would also like to thank my wife for being understanding towards my hobby, and my good friend and fellow enthusiast Kev Moore for his many hours of scanning.

Dave Smith
May 2018

Pathfinder Tours' Cornish Mazey Day excursion skirts the Devon coastline at Cockwood Harbour, led by No.47756 *Royal Mail Tyneside* and No. 46035 *Ixion*, with the return 1Z28 Penzance–Birmingham International on 28 June 2003. The Class 46 failed at Bristol on the outward leg with TPWS problems earlier in the day. It continued the tour assisted by the Class 47.

Loadhaul-liveried Class 56 No. 56118 helps failed EWS No. 60035, working 6F45, the Tees Yard–Skinningrove steel empties, past Hunt Cliff on 10 September 2002.

BR blue Class 50 No. 50007 *Hercules* leads Colas Rail Freight's Class 56 No. 56105 east at Hemington, working 6E07, the Washwood Heath–Boston Docks steel empties, on 17 May 2014.

This was a test run for the Class 50 after an overhaul at the Boden rail workshops, in Washwood Heath, Birmingham.

Direct Rail Services' Class 20s Nos 20302 and 20304 head west at Grange-over-Sands, working 6C52, the Heysham–Sellafield nuclear flasks, on 15 July 2003.

DB Cargo's Class 90s No. 90024 in Malcolm Rail livery and No. 90040 in DB red pass through Atherstone while working 4M25, the Mossend–Daventry (DIRFT) intermodal, on 2 November 2016.

A welcome sight as EWS Class 37s Nos 37174 and 37707 stand in for the usual Class 60 that would be working 6V40, the 06.02 Lackenby–Llanwern loaded steel slabs, as they head south at Hargate on 28 November 2003.

Being led by BR blue Class 20s Nos 20107 and 20096, GBRf No. 20905 and Harry Needles No. 20314 bring up the rear of 7X10, the Banbury Depot Reception–Derby Litchurch Lane S-stock move, passing Clay Mills on 9 March 2017.

The Gloucestershire & Warwickshire Railway's No. 37215 leads GWR steam loco 4-6-0 No. 7903 *Foremarke Hall* on the 12.30 Laverton–Cheltenham service at Hailes Abbey on 29 December 2013 during the Gloucestershire & Warwickshire Railway's mixed traction Christmas gala.

A DRS mixed double with Nos 66433 and 57007 heading north at Church Brampton on the Northampton loop, working a well-loaded 4M71, Purfleet–Daventry (DIRFT), on 1 August 2013.

Two-tone grey No. 73107 *Redhill 1844–1944* and Network Rail-liveried No. 73138, seen heading back to Derby RTC through Wellingborough, are working 1Z26 from Hither Green, with No. 37409 bringing up the rear, on 30 January 2013.

The Nene Valley Railway's September Diesel Gala in 2012 hosted DCR's Class 56s, Nos 56311 and 56091. Here the duo pass Ailsworth, working the 15.30 service from Peterborough to Wansford on 29 September 2012.

Sporting the new Chiltern Railway livery, DRS Class 68s Nos 68013 and 68015 are seen at Stenson Bubble working 6U77, the 13.42 Mountsorrel–Crewe Basford Hall loaded ballast, on 29 August 2015.

On hire to GBRf, BR blue Class 20s Nos 20107 and 20096 head west at East Goscote while working 7X09, the 11.47 Old Dalby–West Ruislip S-stock move, on 15 April 2015. Railfreight-liveried Class 20s Nos 20118 *Saltburn by Sea* and 20132 *Barrow Hill Depot* follow on the rear.

On 3 March 2015, Riviera Trains Nos 47843 *Vulcan* and 47815 *Great Western* pass Blackburn Lane, Knottingley, working 6D31, the 16.12 Drax–Doncaster Decoy. These and two other Class 47s were on hire to GBRf at the time for this working.

Now in their fifty-second year, a pair of Freightliner Class 86s, Nos 86613 and 86628, heads north through Rugby station, working 4M54, the 10.10 Tilbury–Crewe Basford Hall Freightliner, on 10 March 2015.

Both still sporting their original EWS liveries, DB Cargo's Nos 66144 and 66238 head south on the ECML at Joan Croft, working 6D11, the 13.23 Lackenby BSC–Scunthorpe BSC, on 14 April 2015.

Hanson Traction's Class 56s Nos 56312 (ex-56003) and 56311 (ex-56057), on hire to Colas Railfreight, are seen passing Wetmore Farm, Burton-on-Trent, working 6Z57, the Immingham–Washwood Heath loaded steel, on 25 November 2008. The imported steel is used in the production of Toyota cars in Derby.

EWS mixed double as Nos 67004 *Post Haste* and 90040 *The Railway Mission* head alongside the Oxford Canal at Ansty in Warwickshire, working 1S96, the 16.00 London (Willesden Railnet Terminal)–Shieldmuir mail vans, on 17 September 2003.

GB Railfreight electro-diesels Nos 73204 *Janice* and 73206 *Lisa* head away from Egham, working 6G10, the 12.00 engineer's train from Virginia Water to Hoo Junction, on 14 April 2007.

DRS Class 37s Nos 37605 and 37611 pass Easenhall on the West Coast Mainline heading a very short 4Z44, the 06.00 Coatbridge – Daventry International Railfreight Terminal intermodal conveying Malcolm Logistic/ Asda containers, on 17 October 2003.

Due to the WCML being closed for remodelling, here we see Freightliner Class 86s Nos 86623 and 86426 heading south on the ECML at Holme, working 4L97, the 04.57 Trafford Park–Ipswich Yard Freightliner, on 28 September 2002.

On hire to Colas Railfreight, Riviera Trains Nos 47805 *Talisman* and 47769 *Resolve* head south at Holmes House Farm, Bishops Itchington, to the south of Leamington Spa, working a very short 6Z47, the 13.05 Burton-on-Trent Yard–Dollands Moor steel empties, on 22 October 2009.

Passing Wellingborough in sub-zero conditions are EWS Class 60s Nos 60019 *Pathfinder Tours – 30 Years of Rail Touring 1973–2003* and 60091 *An Teallach* working a very late 6V70, the 00.13 Lindsey–Colnbrook train of aviation fuel, on 1 December 2010.

No. 90029, sporting the new DB Schenker colours, and No. 90037 *Spirit of Dagenham*, in the old EWS livery, head south on the WCML at Cathiron, working 4M24, the 06.06 Mossend–Daventry (DIRFT) intermodal, on 12 October 2015.

Large logo Railfreight Class 20s Nos 20118 *Saltburn by Sea* and 20132 *Barrow Hill Depot* pass Bagworth on the Up and Down Burton line, working 7X23, the 09.33 Derby Litchurch Lane–Old Dalby S-stock move, on 16 May 2015. The Underground stock will be at Old Dalby for testing before being delivered to the London Underground.

The daily Bescot–Toton engineer's train can often be seen with more than one loco in its consist, as it is a good way of getting locomotives to and from Toton for service or repair. Here we see Nos 66024 and 60065 *Spirit of Jaguar* heading along the Sheet Stores line at Barrow-on-Trent, working 6D44, the 11.09 from Bescot, on 2 January 2015.

Retro Railtours' The Retro Fenland Explorer heads east past Middle Drove on the approach to March, with DRS Class 37s Nos 37423 and 37605 working 1Z40, the 05.16 Crewe–Great Yarmouth, on 31 August 2013.

A rather shorter than usual 6E38, the 13.54 Colnbrook–Lindsey empty aviation fuel tanks, passes Sharnbrook Junction on the Midland Main Line with DB Schenker Class 60s Nos 60079 and 60010 on 31 July 2013.

Standing in for the usual Class 60, Colas Rail Freight Class 56s Nos 56078 and 56096 pass through Ruscombe on the Western Region main line, working 6V62, the 11.20 Tilbury Riverside–Llanwern steel empties, on 6 December 2014.

On 11 May 2002, Pathfinder Tours ran the Hop 'N Stop railtour, 1Z85, Crewe–Folkestone Harbour, headed by Nos 92007 *Schubert* and 56065, which are seen heading south on the WCML at Ashton in Northamptonshire.

Known as the 'Sugar Liner' due to the consist of Tate & Lyle containers, DR's Nos 57003 and 57009 head north at Church Brampton on the Northampton loop, working 4M71, Tilbury–Daventry (DIRFT), on 21 April 2010.

Thurmaston on the MML plays host to Colas Rail Freight's Class 47s Nos 47739 *Robin of Templecombe* and 47727 *Rebecca* as they head south working 6M08, the 11.50 Boston Docks–Washwood Heath loaded steel, on 5 November 2014. The steel is used for car manufacturing at the Toyota plant in Burnaston, near Derby.

Some of the spoil from the Crossrail project in London was moved by boat across the Thames Estuary from Northfleet in Kent to Wallasea Island in Essex. Large amounts were taken by rail to Northfleet from Willesden. Here we see GBRf electro-diesels Nos 73109 and 73208 passing Longhedge Junction, Battersea, working the return 6M93, the 11.10 Northfleet–Willesden Euroterminal, as a Southern Class 377 passes overhead on 6 March 2014.

With the remains of Didcot power station in the distance, here we see Nos 59101 *Village of Whatley* in Hanson livery and 66015 in EWS colours passing South Moreton while working 6A71, the 11.04 Didcot Yard–Acton TC loaded aggregates, on 22 March 2014.

Old and new Freightliner liveries are contrasted as Nos 86637 and 86605 head south at Gordons Lodge, near Hanslope Junction, working 6L89, the 22.01 Coatbridge–Felixstowe North Freightliner working, on 26 August 2016.

DB Schenker Class 67 No. 67023, still in its EWS livery, leads West Country steam loco No. 34052 south at Cathiron on the West Coast Main Line, working a Crewe Heritage Sidings–Southall loco ECS move, on 12 May 2016.

On hire to GBRf, Class 20s Nos 20314 and 20096 shatter the peace and quiet as they pass Melton Mowbray station while working 7X09, the 11.47 Old Dalby–West Ruislip Tube S-stock move, on 20 April 2016.

The Nene Valley Railway's Spring 2016 Diesel Gala played host to UK Rail Leasing Class 56 No. 56098 *Lost Boys 68–88*, which is seen as it leads resident loco No. 31271 *Stratford 1840–2001* past Ailsworth while working 2E44, the 11.00 Wansford–Peterborough, on 8 April 2016.

Looked on by St Lawrence's Church in Wymington, north Bedfordshire, GBRf No. 66709 *Sorrento*, sporting its Mediterranean Shipping Company livery, and No. 66714 *Cromer Lifeboat* head north while working 6M11, the 13.40 Ferme Park–Wellingborough Yard engineer's train, on 22 July 2013.

EWS Class 31s Nos 31420 in InterCity livery and 31466 in EWS livery arrive at Grain while working 6C78, the 09.19 empty ballast working from Hoo Junction Yard, conveying Seacow wagons for re-loading, on 14 October 1999.

Past Time Rail's 'The Cambrian Growler' stands at Aberystwyth with Class 37s Nos 37114 *City of Worcester* and 37042, waiting with the return 1Z53, the 16.20 back to Milton Keynes, on 22 March 2003. On the return leg of the tour, the locos were changed at Bescot for Mainline blue pairing Nos 37248 and 37372.

A contrast in new and old liveries, as Freightliner Nos 66503 *The Railway Magazine* and, in its new Powerhaul livery, 66504, head south at Somerton in Oxfordshire, working 4O09, the 10.18 Trafford Park–Southampton liner, on 1 May 2013.

Both looking smart in their DB Schenker colours, Class 92s Nos 92042 and 92016 pass through Kensington Olympia in west London, working 4O68, the 03.30 Hams Hall–Dollands Moor intermodal, with the whole consist being made up of Unit45.com containers, on a chilly 9 January 2013.

New and old, as Direct Rail Services' Nos 68010, in Chiltern Railway's livery, and 47828, in the DRS Compass livery, head through the middle road at Northampton station while working 5Z68, the 07.01 Crewe Coal Yard–Willesden Brent, conveying a single Mark 2 coach, on 25 July 2015.

Heading into Sonning Cutting on 13 May 2015, Colas Rail Freight's Class 56s Nos 56105 and 56078, standing in for the usual Class 60, are seen heading west while working 6V62, the 12.01 Tilbury Riverside–Llanwern steel empties, passing Duffield Road, Sonning.

The Nene Valley Railway's Spring Diesel Gala, on 11 April 2015, played host to DB Schenker's Class 60 No. 60001. Here we see the Class 60 with resident loco No. 31271 *Stratford 1840–2001*, passing Ailsworth while working 2M51, the 14.50 Peterborough–Wansford service.

DB Cargo's No. 59001 *Yeoman Endeavour* in Aggregate Industries livery leads No. 66003, still in its EWS livery, through Twyford station on the Up relief, working 7A09, the 07.12 Merehead Quarry–Acton T. C., on 5 May 2016. In the year since this shot was taken, much has changed, with overhead stanchions prominent as they make progress on the electrification of the GWR main line.

A colourful sight in the Leicestershire village of Rearsby as Class 20s Nos 20107 and 20132 pass through while working 7X09, the 11.42 Old Dalby–West Ruislip S-stock move, with Nos 20096 and 20314 bringing up the rear, on 20 April 2016.

Cotswold Rail's Class 47s Nos 47316 *Cam Peak* and 47200 *The Fosse Way* head south at Essendine on the East Coast Main Line, working Pathfinder Tours' The Metallic Maiden (1Z37, Newport–Peterborough) on 18 October 2003. Sadly, No. 47316 was withdrawn in December 2007, being cut up at T. J. Thompsons in Stockton in April 2008. No. 47200 was later withdrawn in December 2007, and was also cut up in May 2008.

On a cold, crisp afternoon on 5 January 2017, Freightliner Nos 70015 and 66598 head west on the Sheet Stores line at Barrow-on-Trent, working 4O95, the 12.13 Leeds–Southampton liner. The Class 66 was Dead in Train in a move to get it to Southampton.

Still in their BR blue liveries, AC electric locomotives Nos 87002 *Royal Sovereign* and 86101 *Sir William A. Stanier FRS* approach Offerd Darcy, working 5Z87, the 13.36 Heaton–Eastleigh ECS, on 15 July 2012.

Under threatening skies, Freightliner GM pairing Nos 66620 and 66525 head north through the Bedfordshire village of Wymington while working 6M92, the 12.42 West Thurrock–Hope Earles Sidings cement empties, on 21 April 2012.

The then daily 7C20 (the 08.12 Sellafield–Drigg low level nuclear waste trip) passes Seascale Golf Course on the Cumbrian coast with DRS Crompton's Nos 33025 and 33027 on a pleasant 16 July 2003.

Crossing the River Nene as they arrive at Wansford, GBRf electro-diesels Nos 73209 *Alison* and 73206 *Lisa* arrive with 1M49, the 13.23 service from Peterborough. This was during the Nene Valley Railway's Diesel Gala, on 17 September 2005.

Both in their early BR green liveries, Boston Dock's resident shunters D2112 (ex-03112) and D3871 (ex-08704) cross the swing bridge on 13 October 2006 with an empty set of Lafarge discharge wagons, destined for Mountsorrel in Leicestershire.

Main line preserved locos Nos 50031 *Hood*, owned by the Class 50 Fund, and 50049 *Defiance*, owned by Project Defiance, head out of Didcot at Didcot North Junction, working Pathfinder Tours' Harrogate Hoovers, 1Z27, the Reading–York via Harrogate, on 13 July 2002.

An English, Welsh & Scottish mixed double sees Nos 60047 and 37670 departing Milford Sidings with a set of empty MGRs for Ayr in Scotland – a long-distance working via the Settle & Carlisle line – on 2 October 1999.

With DRS Class 47s Nos 47818 and 47802 leading, 1Z62, the 05.50 Edinburgh–Southampton Eastern Docks 'Cruise Saver Express', is seen here passing Warkworth, to the south of Banbury, on 16 October 2011.

Colas Rail Freight's 6V62, the 11.20 Tilbury Riverside–Llanwern Exchange Sidings steel empties, is seen waiting in Challow Loop on the Great Western main line with Class 56s Nos 56113 and 56087 on 9 August 2014. From Tilbury, the steel is exported to mainland Europe.

GBRf Class 66 pairing Nos 66731 *Interhub* GB and 66717 *Good Old Boy* head east at Langham Junction while working 4L22, the 14.35 Hams Hall–Felixstowe Liner, on 30 June 2014.

With Ratcliffe Power Station prominent in the distance, DRS Class 57s Nos 57002 and 57010 pass Castle Donnington on the Sheet Stores Junction to Stenson Junction branch line, working 6U77, the 13.42 Mountsorrel–Crewe Basford Hall loaded ballast, on 30 June 2014.

With the now closed London Brickworks in the distance at Stewartby, EWS Class 37s Nos 37114 *City of Worcester* and 37682 *Hartlepool Pipe Mill* await the signal to depart Forders Sidings while working 4D51, the 10.52 Binliner train to Cricklewood, on 10 April 2001.

Heading north out of Roade Cutting at Courteenhall, EWS electric locos Nos 92025 *Oscar Wilde* and 92007 *Schubert* head down the Northampton Loop, working 4M76, the 12.20 Dollands Moor–Trafford Park intermodal, on 4 April 2001.

Shattering the peace and quiet of the Yorkshire Moors, BR blue Sulzer pairing Nos 27001 and 26024 climb up to Goathland at Thomason Foss on the North Yorkshire Moors Railway, working the 11.45 Grosmont–Pickering service during the line's diesel gala on 13 May 2005.

With the flowering Rose Bay Willowherb in full bloom, BR green D5528/31110 and Dutch-liveried No. 31154 wait to depart Lowestoft with A1A Charters' 'Fairwell Arms II' leg of the tour to London Liverpool Street on 21 August 1999. The tour started from King's Cross with the Class 31s, and from Norwich Loadhaul pairing Nos 37713 and 37513 took the tour forward to Lowestoft.

The Gloucestershire & Warwickshire Railway's 2013 Christmas Mixed Traction Gala sees freshly painted Class 24 D5018/24081 and steam locomotive GWR 2-8-0 No. 2807 heading south at Didbrook while working 1C10, the 10.00 Toddington to Cheltenham service, on 29 December 2013. The steam locomotive dates back to 1905, which is one of the oldest survivors of G. J. Churchward's era as CME of the GWR.

With the May trees in full blossom, Colas Rail Freight's Class 56 No. 56105 screams through Muston with BR blue Nos 50007 *Hercules* and 47739 *Robin of Templecombe* on the return 6M08, the 15.12 Boston–Washwood Heath loaded steel, on 17 May 2014. Earlier in the day the Class 50 led a test run to Boston after an overhaul, which was successful.

Heading out of Challow Loop, EWS Class 66 No. 66092 leads Euro Cargo's No. 66212, heading west on the GW main line working 6V13, the 08.31 Dollands Moor–Margam steel empties, on 29 March 2014. With the steel wagons returning from Dunkirk in northern France, this is a good way of returning Euro Cargo's locos for maintenance in the UK.

It is always good to see preserved diesels on the main line. Here we see two Class 20 examples heading north at Rushton, Northamptonshire, with No. 20182 in London Transport livery and No. 20142 in BR blue working 6D02, the 11.28 Wellingborough Yard–Mountsorrel empties, on 22 January 2014. The locos were on hire to GBRf to cover their shortfall of motive power.

DB Cargo's No. 90039, still in EWS livery, and No. 90018, in its new DB Schencker livery, head south at Atherstone in Warwickshire on the West Coast Main Line, working 4M26, the 06.06 Mossend–Daventry (DIRFT) intermodal, on 28 September 2015.

With Wembley Stadium closed for a rebuild, and the 2001 FA Cup Final between Arsenal and Liverpool being played at the Millennium Stadium in Cardiff, numerous Footex trains were being used. Here we see Class 37s Nos 37029 and 37038 heading west at Marshfields, working 1Z12, Liverpool Lime Street–Cardiff Central, on 12 May. Liverpool won 2-1.

With Nos 47756 *Royal Mail Tyneside* and 46035 *Ixion*, Pathfinder Tours' Cornish Mazey Day Excursion (1Z46, 04.55 Birmingham International–Penzance) is seen heading along the sea wall at Starcross, in Devon, on 28 June 2003. The Class 47 was added to the train at Bristol as No. 46035 had a TPWS fault and was unable to lead.

BR large logo Class 50s Nos 50031 *Hood* and 50049 *Defiance* head south on the Midland Main Line at Oakley in Bedfordshire, with Pathfinder Tours' The Alton Observer (1Z50, 05.55 Sheffield–Alton), on 9 October 2004. At London Victoria EWS Class 60 No. 60001 was added and led the train to Alresford.

Freightliner Class 86 locos Nos 86628 and 86607 pass through Ipswich station on the start of their long journey north, working 4M88, the 09.32 Felixstowe–Crewe Basford Hall Freightliner working, on 2 February 2016.

Electro-diesels Nos 73962 *Dick Mabbutt* and 73965, both in GBRf livery, head north through the Bedfordshire village of Souldrop while working 1Z80, the 13.56 Dollands Moor–Derby RTC Test Train, on 6 June 2016.

In readiness for the upcoming Rail Head Treatment season, DRS Class 57s Nos 57002 and 57012 head through North Fen, Little Downham, while working 6Z50, the 10.15 York Thrall Europa–Stowmarket RHTT, on 29 September 2015.

With Colas Rail Freight acquiring ten Class 60 locomotives from DB Schenker in April 2014, one of its main workings using the class is 6E38, the 13.54 Colnbrook–Lindsey Oil Refinery, conveying aviation fuel for Heathrow Airport. Here we see No. 60021 helping failed classmate No. 60096 north at Irchester on the Midland Main Line, on the return working, on 15 May 2015.

Making light work of its short engineer's train, Colas Rail Freight's Type 5s Nos 56302 and 56094 pass Branston, south of Burton-on-Trent, on a cold, crisp 2 February 2014, working train 6Z47, the 09.59 Burton Wetmore Sidings–Taunton Fairwater Yard.

On 11 January 2014, Pathfinder Tours' The Deviationer (1Z20, 06.22 Crewe–Ely Papworth Sidings) is seen passing Harrowden Junction, to the north of Wellingborough, with DRS Class 20s Nos 20302 and 20305 leading and with No. 37194 on the rear.

EWS Class 37s Nos 37417 *Richard Trevithick* and 37401 head out into the Fens at Whittlesea on 26 April 2008, working Pathfinder Tours' The Grays Church Elegy (1Z37, 06.00 Crewe–London Fenchurch Street).

Both Boston Dock resident shunters, D2112 (No. 03112) and D3871 (No. 08704), in their original green liveries, are seen in Boston Docks on 13 October 2006 after shunting the return self-discharge wagons from Mountsorrel in Leicestershire. The two shunters take the train out of the docks complex and over the swing bridge into the Sleaford Sidings, where a main line loco will take the train forward.

Seen arriving at Stud Farm Quarry in Leicestershire on 20 October 2003 are EWS Class 37s No. 37375 in Mainline blue livery without decals, and No. 37707 (ex-37001), in EWS house colours, with 6Z50 ballast empties from Crewe Basford Hall. Once the locos have run round the train will be loaded and then returned to Crewe with ballast for the virtual quarry at Basford Hall Yard.

With the West Coast Main Line closed for engineering, Virgin Trains No. 47805 *Pride of Toton* drags electric loco No. 90009 *The Economist* on a diverted 1G23, the 10.30 London Euston–Wolverhampton service, through Whitacre Junction on 2 June 2002.

A pair of DB Schenker Class 66s, both still in their EWS livery, head along the Great Western Main Line at Denchworth on 11 January 2014, working the return 6V13, the 08.31 Dollands Moor–Margam steel empties.

The Gloucestershire & Warwickshire Railway's March 2004 Diesel Gala sees both resident locos Nos 24081, in BR blue, and Class 14 D9539 in early green livery, exit Winchcombe Tunnel, working the 14.40 Cheltenham–Toddington service, on 13 March 2004.

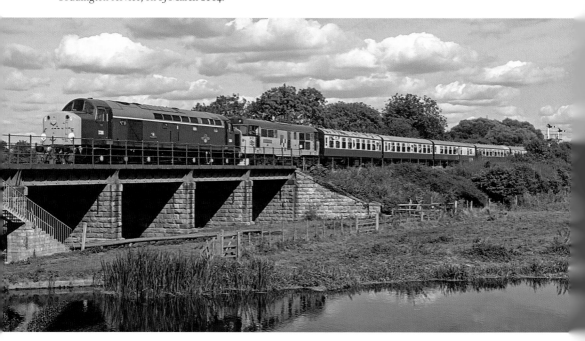

Looking splendid in BR green, Class 40 D306 *Atlantic Conveyor* and No. 31271 *Stratford 1840–2001* cross the River Nene as they arrive at Wansford while working 2M50, the 13.59 service from Peterborough, during the Nene Valley Railway's Autumn Diesel Gala on 17 September 2005.

On 3 March 2008, EWS Class 67s Nos 67019 and 67027 cross over the River Nene at Irchester on the Midland Main Line while working 5Z67, the 09.10 Toton–Old Oak Common ECS.

GBRf electro-diesel loco No. 73207, in BR large logo livery, is seen on yard shunting duties in March Whitemoor Yard with Freightliner No. 66545 after arriving with 6Y50, the High Output Ballast Cleaner engineers' train from Sharnbrook, on 1 September 2009. In January 2015 the Class 73 became No. 73971, and is now used for Caledonian Sleeper duties in Scotland.

A DRS treble sees Class 37s Nos 37059 and 37423 hauling Class 47 No. 47712 Dead in Train and a set of newly imported Fastline Freight coal wagons through Wellingborough on a Wembley Yard–Chaddesden Sidings wagon move on 21 August 2008.

Hired in by Colas Rail Freight, Riviera Trains' Class 47s Nos 47848 *Titan Star* and 47839 *Pegasus* pass through Bentley Heath on 10 September 2009 while working 6Z48, the 13.05 steel empties from Burton Yard to Dollands Moor, for imported steel from France.

King Sutton in west Northamptonshire plays host to EWS Class 37s Nos 37667 *Meldon Quarry Centenary* and 37895, which are working a very short 6M65, the 18.19 Didcot Yard–Carlisle Yard Enterprise, on a pleasant evening on 7 June 2004.

On 29 April 2013, West Coast Railways Cromptons Nos 33029 *Glen Roy* and 33207 *Jim Martin* head north on the Northampton Loop, at Church Brampton, while working 5Z57, the 13.00 Southall–Carnforth ECS.

Crossing the River Esk on Eskmeals Viaduct in Cumbria is a quartet of DRS Class 20s. Nos 20315 and 20307, hauling Nos 20314 and 20310 DIT, are working 6K73, the 15.35 Sellafield–Crewe flasks, on a warm 16 July 2003.

With the rosebay willowherb in full bloom, Colas Rail Freight's Class 47s Nos 47727 *Rebecca* and 47749 *Demelza* are seen north of King Sutton working 6Z48, the 13.05 Burton Yard–Dollands Moor steel empties, on 2 July 2009.

Heading north alongside the Oxford Canal at Ansty in Warwickshire, Hanson Traction's Class 56s Nos 56312 (ex-56003) and 56311 (ex-56057) head a block train of Norfolkline intermodal containers, the 4Z91 Dollands Moor–Hams Hall working, on 10 September 2009.

Headed by EWS Class 67s Nos 67001 and 67016, Past Time Rail's The York Flyer, 1Z27, the 05.50 Taunton–York, heads north at Stenson Junction on 27 August 2005.

Two of Freightliner's veteran electric locos, Nos 86639 and 86612, head south over the River Stour Viaduct at Manningtree while working a colourful 4M88, the 09.32 Felixstowe–Crewe Basford Hall Freightliner, on 28 January 2016.

On hire to GBRf, Class 20s Nos 20314 and 20096 lead classmates Nos 20132 *Barrow Hill Depot* and 20107 past the A607 Syston Bypass, working 6M24, the 08.46 Derby–Old Dalby barrier move, on 20 April 2016.

Conveying a lengthy train of new concrete sleepers, EWS Class 37s No. 37042, in house colours, and a tatty-looking Mainline grey-liveried No. 37890 head down to Rycroft Junction while working 7G22, the 13.01 Washwood Heath RMC Sidings–Bescot Departmental, on 24 June 2003.

Taking a break from their usual East Midlands coal duties are two of EWS's well turned out locos, No. 56115 *Barry Needham* and No. 58037 *Worksop Depot*. The former leads the latter south at Isham on the Midland Main Line while working 1Z56, the 06.22 Worksop–Margate Worksop Invicta Railtour, on 30 June 2001.

GBRf's hired in Type 4s, No. 47847 looking smart in its BR large logo livery and No. 47843 *Vulcan* in Riviera Oxford Blue, open up after a signal check at High Eggborough, working 4D93, the 09.41 Doncaster Decoy–Drax empty gypsum containers, on 14 April 2015.

Old and new locomotive liveries are contrasted as the GM pairing No. 66725 *Sunderland*, in GBRf's first colours, and No. 66763, in the company's new house livery, head south at Catholme, near Wichnor Junction, while working 6K50, the 15.13 Toton North Yard–Crewe Basford Hall engineer's train, on 30 April 2015.

Rounding the curve at Old Linslade on the West Coast Main Line, DB Schenker's Class 90s Nos 90018 *The Pride of Bellshill* and 90020 *Collingwood* head a very lightly loaded 6M76, the 21.46 Mossend Down Yard–Wembley Yard working, on 12 August 2016.

6M76, the 21.29 Mossend–Wembley Enterprise train, passes through Northampton station on 14 April 2003, headed by Class 92s Nos 92026 *Britten* and 92042 *Honegger*. The downturn in traffic can be seen clearly in the previous picture, which was taken thirteen years later.

Fragonset Railways Class 31s Nos 31128 *Charybdis* and 31459 *Cerberus* cross the River Nene as they arrive at Peterborough with the return 1Z44, the 16.42 St James Day Tripper, Norwich–Preston railtour, on 6 September 2003. Sadly, the spot hire company, formed in 1997, only lasted three more years after this shot was taken, with its locos moving on to other companies in 2006.

Fresh from the paint shops, DRS Class 20 No. 20310 leads classmate No. 20314 out of the Sellafield complex in Cumbria while on shunting duties after arriving with 6C53, the 06.33 working from Crewe, on 16 July 2003.

Passing the site of the exchange sidings at Glendon East on the Kettering–Corby line, Freightliner GM pairing Nos 66511 and 66620 pass with 6L87, the 12.35 Earles Sidings–West Thurrock loaded cement, on 17 July 2012. Loco No. 66612 was DIT on a move south to get the loco to Dagenham Yard for a scrap metal flow to Cardiff.

Colas Rail Freight's green Class 37 No. 37057 leads GBRf electro-diesels Nos 73962 *Dick Mabbutt* and 73963 *Janice* over the River Nene at Irchester, working 1Q79, the 14.45 Cricklewood Depot–Derby RTC test train, on 7 May 2017. The Class 37 was sent light engine from Derby as both Class 73s run low on fuel in the capital.

Fresh from their repaint/overhaul, Fastline Freight's Class 56s Nos 56303 (ex-56125) and 56301 (ex-56045) arrive at Rugby with 6Z56 from Doncaster on 23 May 2006. This was a test run for the two locos, conveying a slinger rail carrying set.

New and old Freightliner liveries contrast as Class 47 No. 47289, in Freightliner grey, leads classmate No. 47150, in the new Freightliner green livery, south through Elford while working 4O31, the 14.33 Leeds–Southampton Freightliner, on 31 January 2001.

Making easy work of their light load, DRS Class 37s Nos 37612 and 37229 *Jonty Jarvis 8-12-1998 to 18-3-2005* pass through Roade in Northamptonshire, working 4L46, the 11.18 Ditton–Purfleet intermodal, on 5 June 2006. Sadly, the Piano Forte supplies factory behind the locos, which manufactured car components, has since closed and been demolished to make way for a housing development.

The peaceful setting of Darnholm, on the North Yorkshire Railway, played host to Brunswick green No. 50007 *Sir Edward Elgar,* named to commemorate the 150th anniversary of GWR, and No. 50033 *Glorious,* in BR large logo, on 24 April 2004 while working the 09.50 Grosmont–Pickering service during the line's diesel gala.

A mixed trio, as Ian Riley & Son (E) Limited Locomotive Engineers Class 37s No. 37197, in two-tone green livery, and No. 37038, in Civil Engineer's livery, lead Riviera Trains Class 47 No. 47839, in Oxford Blue, past the splendid Stokesay Castle to the south of Craven Arms while working 1Z37, the 12.20 Crewe–Cardiff Central Rugby special, on 22 February 2003. The Class 47 was in the train to supply ETH.

The Nene Valley Railway's September 2005 Diesel Gala sees Class 14s (Teddy Bears) D9516 and No. 9520 passing Mill Lane, Castor, while working 2E48, the 12.01 Wansford–Peterborough, on 19 September.

Rounding the curve at Slindon, Staffordshire, a pair of Freightliner Class 86s, Nos 86614 and 86605, heads north while working 4M87, the 11.13 Felixstowe to Trafford Park Freightliner working, on 5 May 2017.

DRS Class 20s Nos 20305 *Gresty Bridge* and 20308 make for a rare sight on the Midland Main Line at Kettering North Junction while working 6Z20, the 10.30 Chaddesden Sidings–West Ealing Plasser Works, hauling Network Rail's new ballast regulator DR77904, on 23 February 2015.

Two of GBRf's electro-diesels, Nos 73209 *Alison* and 73205 *Jeanette*, are seen passing Rusham Crossing, in Egham, working 6G13, the 14.00 Virginia Water–Hoo Junction engineer's train, on 14 April 2007.

On hire to Colas Rail Freight, two Riviera blue Class 47s, Nos 47848 *Titan* and 47839 *Pegasus,* pass Castle Bromwich while working 6Z48, the 13.05 Burton Yard–Dollands Moor steel empties, on 10 September 2009.

After trying and failing twice before, Pathfinder Tours' The Clacton Avoider (1Z71, 08.45 Crewe–Clacton) heads south at Warkworth, to the south of Banbury, with EWS Class 56s Nos 56018 and 56032 on 18 May 2003. The first attempt was on 26 August 2002 and was named The Bone Breaker, terminating at Walton-on-Naze after it collided with the buffers. The second attempt on 22 October 2002, The Gratis Grids, the headboard of which is carried in this picture, only made it from Crewe to Stafford owing to atrocious weather conditions.

With its lengthy consist of forty Tope wagons loaded with spoil, EWS-liveried Class 37 No. 37885 and tatty No. 37255 in Civil Engineer's livery wait to return to Toton Yard in the East Midlands from Finedon Road, Wellingborough, where they are pictured on 26 September 1999.

Still in EWS livery, DB Schenker's Class 90s Nos 90037 *Spirit of Dagenham* and 90024, in First Scotrail livery, head north at Church Brampton while working a late-running 6B41, the 11.43 Wembley–Daventry (DIRFT) cargo vans conveying bottled water from France, on 20 January 2015.

Looking very smart in their Railfreight grey liveries, Class 20s Nos 20118 *Saltburn on the Sea* and 20132 *Barrow Hill Depot* pass Frisby in rural Leicestershire on 5 November 2014 while working 7X09, the 11.22 Old Dalby–Derby Adtranz London Underground S-stock move, with Class 20s Nos 20107 and 20096 in BR blue on the rear.

A welcome sight on 19 November 2013 as a DB Schenker trio with three different classes of locomotives sees No. 66145 leading No. 60059 *Swinden Dalesman* and No. 67008 past Chellaston while working 6D44, the 11.09 Bescot–Toton engineer's train.

Pathfinder Tours' The Crompton Collier (1Z90, Crewe–Gedling Colliery) pass the old wagon repair shops at Burton-on-Trent, with Class 33s Nos 33021 *Eastleigh* in red and 33103 in green on the Crewe–Derby leg on 20 November 1999.

Direct Rail Services Class 20s Nos 20309 and 20313 pass through Warrington Bank Quay while working 6F20, the 08.23 (Tuesdays and Fridays only) Sellafield–Sandbach empty nitric acid tanks, on 11 May 2001. The acid is used at Sellafield to dissolve spent nuclear fuel rods.

With the West Coast Main Line closed for remodelling, most of their Royal Mail workings were diverted onto the Midland Main Line. Here we see No. 47739 *Resourceful* dragging electric loco No. 92012 *Thomas Hardy* and 325 units Nos 011, 003 and 012, while heading south at Harrowden Junction with a Crewe–Willesden working on 26 August 2003.

On 16 September 2003, EWS GM pairing Nos 66140 and 66149 pass Whitacre Junction while working a Daw Mill Colliery–Didcot Power Station loaded train of coal. Since this photograph was taken, Daw Mill Colliery has closed.

Pathfinder Tours' The Metallic Maiden (1Z37, Newport–Peterborough) heads along the Sheet Stores line at Barrow upon Trent on 18 October 2003, with Mainline blue No. 37375 leading classmate No. 37707 (ex-37001). At Toton the Class 37s were replaced by Class 56 No. 56083 to Doncaster, where Class 47s Nos 47316 and 47200 took the train forward to Peterborough, before Class 60 No. 60005 headed back to Toton.

6D65, the 10.07 Doncaster–Immingham Enterprise, heads east at New Barnetby on 26 June 2001 with an EWS combo of locos comprising of No. 60015 *Bow Fell* leading Nos 56041 and 66011. This working was a good way of moving locomotives to Immingham from Doncaster after maintenance/service.

BR two-tone green Class 47 D1705 (47117) *Sparrowhawk* and No. 47714, in faded Anglian livery, are seen arriving at Rothley while working 2A24, the 13.00 Loughborough–Leicester service, on 11 September 2009, during the Great Central Railway's Autumn Diesel Gala.

Looking very smart after their recent repaints, preserved Class 56s No. 56057 *British Fuels*, in BR large logo livery, and No. 56003, in Loadhaul livery, pass Ailsworth working 2M96, the 15.00 Peterborough–Wansford service, during the Nene Valley Railway's Autumn Diesel Gala on 6 October 2006.

Two of GBRf's Class 66s, Nos 66704 *Colchester Power Signal Box* and 66713 *Forest City*, are seen nearing their destination as they arrive at Wellingborough while working 6M11, the 13.40 Ferme Park–Wellingborough Yard loaded train of ballast, on 16 May 2011.

Warkworth, to the south of Banbury, plays host to DRS Class 37s Nos 37682 and 37409 *Lord Hinton*, as they head south while working a colourful 5Z47 ECS from Crewe to Eastleigh on 8 March 2011.

Two of the Gloucestershire & Warwickshire Railway's long-time residents, No. 24081 and D8137 (20137), head south at Hails Abbey while working the 10.20 service from Toddington to Cheltenham during the line's diesel gala on 13 March 2004.

Not long into their journey, two Riviera Class 47s hired in by Colas Rail, Nos 47848 *Titan Star* and 47839 *Pegasus*, pass Branston while working 6Z48, the 13.05 Burton-on-Trent Yard–Dollands Moor covered steel empties, on 10 September 2009.

Freightliner's locomotive/wagon move from Barden Hill to Crewe Basford Hall for repair/exams sees GM pairing Nos 66552 *Maltby Raider* and 66546 passing Rycroft on the Sutton Park line, working 6Z98 with two HIA wagons in its consist, on 24 April 2008.

Electro-diesels Class 73 No. 73205 *Jeanette* and classmate No. 73209 *Alison* head a Derby RTC–Tonbridge Yard test train, with Network Rail's Nos 73212 and 73213 on the rear, and are seen as they pass Harrowden Junction on 4 December 2007.

On a dull and damp 24 February 2007, Class 56s No. 56003, in Loadhaul livery, and 56098, in Railfreight grey livery, head into Orton Mere station, on the Nene Valley Railway, with an engineer's train from Wansford.

Two of Harry Needle Railroad Co.'s Class 20s, Nos 20905 and 20901 in Railfreight grey livery, rest between duties in Wellingborough Yard on 4 April 2010. The locos were hired in by GBRf and were used for S-stock moves from Old Dalby. These locos have since been outshopped in GBRf's blue with mustard yellow cabs and orange cantrail plus sole bar stripes, and 'GB Railfreight part of Europorte' branding.

Old and new DRS liveries are contrasted as Class 37s Nos 37607 and 37059 head north on the Northampton loop through Great Brington, working 4M71, the 10.53 Tilbury–Daventry (DIRFT) sugar liner, on 2 June 2010.

An EWS trio of Class 66s sees No. 66604 leading Nos 66194 and 66003 and heading south at Harrowden Junction on the Midland Main Line, working 6B42, the Toton Yard–Acton engineer's train, on 5 August 2006.

New and old Freightliner liveries are seen as Class 86s Nos 86610 and 86637 head north through Manningtree station while working 6L89, the 22.00 Coatbridge–Ipswich Yard Freightliner, on 12 August 2008.

A colourful Pathfinder Tours London/The Marshes Marauder (1Z48, 15.38 Dungeness–Crewe) is seen as it passes Westbrook Farm crossing, near Lydd on the Dungeness branch, with Class 73s Nos 73133 *The Bluebell Railway* and 73131, with No. 33021 on the rear, on 7 April 2001.

Comberford's crossing, Hademore, on the West Coast Main Line, is the setting for DRS Type 3s Nos 37259 and 37610 *The Malcolms Group* as they head south working 4Z44, the 06.00 Coatbridge–Daventry (DIRFT) intermodal, on 20 October 2003. With the West Coast Main Line upgrade, this piece of line is now four track, and the crossing has been replaced with a footbridge.

Both in Freightliner's early grey livery, Class 47s Nos 47367 and 47290 pass through the middle road of Newport station while working 6V16, the 09.46 Millbrook–Cardiff Pengam Freightliner, on 6 November 1999.

A busy scene at Lowestoft on 21 August 1999 sees Loadhaul pairing Nos 37713 and 37513 making way for Class 31s Nos 31110 and 31154 on the return leg of AIA Charters' Fairwell Arms tour, heading back to London Liverpool Street.

With the low winter sun setting at Harrowden Junction, Railfreight grey-liveried Class 20s Nos 20901 and 20905 lead BR blue No. 20042 and Railfreight large logo No. 20227 north, working 6M11, the Neasden–Derby Litchurch Lane barrier move, on 16 January 2012.

Courteenhall, on the Northampton loop, sees Freightliner GM double Nos 66564 and 66541 making easy work of the lightly loaded 4L97, the 05.19 Trafford Park–Felixstowe Freightliner, on 7 May 2013.

Spitfire Railtours' 1Z44, Crewe–Weymouth, heads south at Somerton, to the south of Aynho Junction, led by DRS Class 37s Nos 37602 and 37609, on a warm and pleasant 23 May 2009.

Still looking fresh after a re-paint, DB Schenker's No. 59204 leads No. 66207, in the old EWS livery, north through Theale station on the Berks & Hants while working 7A09, the 07.12 Merehead–Acton loaded aggregates, on 1 August 2013. Since this shot was taken, electrification masts have been erected in readiness for the forthcoming electrification to Bedwyn.

Virgin Trains No. 47810 *Porterbrook* drags electric loco No. 87001 *Royal Scot* through Whitacre Junction in Warwickshire while working a diverted 1G25, the 10.50 Euston–Wolverhampton service, on 21 June 2003.

On the weekend of Friday 23 April to Sunday 25 April 2004, the North Yorkshire Moors Railway hosted a diesel gala. Here we see Class 50s Nos 50007 *Sir Edward Elgar* and 50033 *Glorious* arriving at Levisham while working the 15.50 service from Grosmont on 25 April.

Heading south on the West Coast Main Line at Colton, to the north of Rugeley, are DB Cargo's Class 90s No. 90024, sporting its Malcolm Rail livery, and No. 90018 *The Pride of Bellshill*, which are working 4M25, the 06.07 Mossend–Daventry (DIRFT) intermodal, on 9 March 2017.

Virgin Trains Class 87s Nos 87010 *King Arthur* and 87022 *Lew Adams the Black Prince* head south at Wilson's Crossing, Kingsthorpe, on the Northampton loop, while working 1A67, the 14.19 Wolverhampton–Milton Keynes service, on 23 August 2003.

The Midland Main Line at Harrowden Junction sees DRS Type 3s Nos 37510 and 37667 heading south while working 4Z90, the 08.37 Tyne Dock–Sheerness long-distance scrap metal flow, on 21 April 2010.

With engineering work taking place in Ipswich Tunnel, the Great Eastern Main Line was closed from 11 July to 5 September 2004. With some services being diverted, here we see Anglia-liveried Nos 47714 and 86246 *Royal Anglian Regiment* with ex-Virgin-liveried No. 90011 working 1G09, the 06.30 Norwich–London Liverpool Street service, south at Littlebury on 29 July 2004.

In happier days, green Class 37s Nos 37197 and 37261 pass Carters House on the North Yorkshire Moors Railway on 25 April 2004, working a Grosmont–Pickering service. Sadly, No. 37197 was cut up by DRS in 2012, and No. 37261 was stripped for component recovery by the same company. No. 37261 has since secured a happier future, being preserved by the Scottish Class 37 Group and the Bo'ness Diesel Group.

Devon & Cornwall Railways Grids Nos 56303 and 56301 head away from Royston while working 6Z17, the 12.28 Foxton Exchange Sidings–Wembley Euro Ops Centre spoil empties, on 6 November 2017.

With both locos in Freightliner's early grey livery, electric locos Nos 86606 and 86611 *Airey Neave* pass Cathiron, to the north of Rugby, while working a colourful 4L75, the 10.14 Trafford Park–Ipswich Yard Freightliner, on 17 September 2003.

With DB Cargo's No. 66135 failing at Bletchley, Class 60 No. 60066, in its silver livery and 'Drax – Powering Tomorrow' branding, was sent light engine from Toton TMD to assist. Here the pair head north at Rushton while working 6H03, the 12.27 Bletchley–Toton, on 30 September 2017.

Rail Operations Group briefly took charge of the Willesden–Barrington spoil working. Here we see Type 4s Nos 47815 and 47848 as they pass Shepreth, working 6T02, the 11.28 Barrington Unloading Pad–Wembley Euro Ops Centre spoil empties, on 23 November 2017.

BR blue Class 50s Nos 50031 *Hood* and 50049 *Defiance* pass the remains of Wellingborough No. 2 Steam Shed, working a colourful mixed ECS from York to Old Oak Common, on 23 September 2002.

Fragonset Railways Class 31s Nos 31128 *Charybdis* and 31459 *Cerberus* are seen departing Newark working the St James Day Tripper railtour (1Z43, Preston–Norwich) on 6 September 2003.

The Worksop Open Day Committee railtour, The Worksop Riviera, heads south at Kingsbury brickworks with Loadhaul Grids Nos 56118 and 56107 while working 1Z56, the 05.40 Worksop–Paignton tour, on 3 August 2003.

DRS Class 37s Nos 37612 and 37059 pass Brockhall, north of Weedon, working a lightly loaded 4L46, the 11.18 Ditton–Purfleet intermodal, on 25 May 2006.

Virgin Trains Class 47 No. 47810 *Porterbrook* drags Railfreight Distribution-liveried Class 90 No. 90023 past Saltley Viaduct while working 1G16, the 06.50 London Euston–Wolverhampton service, on 21 June 2003.

Freshly painted in Harry Needle's colours, Class 20s Nos 20311 and 20314 head north through Wellingborough while working 6Z20, the 12.21 Ruislip–Derby Eches Park barrier move, with BR blue Class 20s Nos 20107 and 20096 on the rear, on 3 October 2012.

Still in their EWS liveries, Class 90s Nos 90020 *Collingwood* and 90035 wait to depart while working 6X77, the 13.58 Dagenham Down Reception–Mossend Down Yard train of Ford cars and vans, on 5 October 2017.

Built for use on the Jubilee Line Extension, London Underground's German-built Schoma locomotives Nos 3 *Claire* and 6 *Debora* are seen bringing a loaded train of ballast into West Ruislip Yard on 20 October 2015.

Transrail grey Class 60 No. 60034 leads Loadhaul Class 56 No. 56100 south at Hargate, to the north of Burton, with a loaded Merry-Go-Round coal from Toton to Drakelow on 22 September 2001. Sadly, Drakelow C Power Station closed on 31 March 2003.

On hire to Devon & Cornwall Railways, Class 56s Nos 56301 and 56081 head 6Z17, the 11.30 Foxton Exchange Sidings–Wembley Euro Ops Centre spoil empties, south through Wellham Green as Virgin Trains East Coast service 1A25, the 10.45 Leeds–London King's Cross, is about to overtake on 21 October 2017.

To commemorate the 60th anniversary of the Class 31s, the Nene Valley Railway held a gala in October. Here we see No. 5580 (31162), in BR blue, leading classmate No. 31466, in EWS livery, into Orton Mere station while working 2E45, the 10.02 Wansford–Peterborough service, on 14 October 2017.

Past Time Rail's The Spinning State VI, 1Z54, the 09.05 London Euston–Preston, negotiates Hatton Bank with EWS Class 37 No. 37109 leading Mainline blue classmate No. 37216 on 1 March 2003.

Mixed liveries sees EWS Class 47s Nos 47784 *Condover Hall* in RES, and 47793 *St Augustin* in house colours, heading away from Harlesden with a TPO ECS working to Euston Downside Carriage Maintenance Depot on 27 March 2003.

Freightliner veteran electric Class 86s Nos 86604 and 86612 head south at Church Brampton while working 4Z57, the 13.06 Daventry (DIRFT)–Tilbury Freightliner, on a very cold 8 December 2010.

A GBRf mixed combo sees No. 66713 *Forest City* leading Nos 66410 (ex-DRS), 73207 (in BR large logo) and 66702 *Blue Lightning* into Wellingborough while working a very short 6M09, the 13.40 Ferme Park–Wellingborough Yard engineer's train, on 4 March 2010.

The GB Railfreight Yard at Wellingborough played host to a colourful quartet of Class 20s on 16 April 2010, as two-tone grey Nos 20901 and 20905, BR green No. 20189 and BR blue No. 20142 are seen stabled with an engineer's train.

Making easy work of their light load, Class 31s Nos 31459 and 31271 *Stratford 1840–2001* head away from Orton Mere while working 2E42, the 08.40 Wansford–Peterborough service, during the Nene Valley Railway's Class 31 60th anniversary event, on 14 October 2017.

An EWS treble sees Class 47 No. 47773 *The Queen Mother* leading Class 90s Nos 90018 and 90032, with electric units Nos 325002 and 325009 in tow, while working 5A98, the 11.18 Crewe–Willesden Railnet empty rail units, south at Easenhall on 5 November 2003.

Catching the early morning sun, Pathfinder Tours' Bicester Baseline (1Z37, Crewe–Oxford) passes Grimsbury to the north of Banbury, headed by EWS Class 37s Nos 37308 and 37057 *Viking*, on 17 November 2002.

Freightliner Class 66s Nos 66601 *The Hope Valley* and 66951 head past at Souldrop in Bedfordshire while working a very short 6M84, the 15.04 Dagenham–Hope Earles Sidings cement empties, on 14 July 2017.

With Network Rail's No. 86901 in Rugby Carriage Sidings looking on, Freightliner Nos 86610 and 86627 haul DIT No. 57007 *Freightliner Bond* past with 4L75, the 10.04 Trafford Park–Ipswich Yard Freightliner through working, on 4 August 2005.

Virgin Trains Class 47 No. 47826 *Springburn* in Intercity livery and Class 90 No. 90007 *Lord Stamp* pass through Northampton working 1A55, the 11.15 Liverpool Lime St–London Euston service, on 17 December 2007.

Freightliner's Veteran Class 47 No. 47816 hauls Class 66 No. 66525 Dead in Train north at Ashton in Northamptonshire on the West Coast Main Line while working 4M26, the 14.41 Dagenham–Crewe Gresty Bridge Ford cars, on 28 June 2005.

BR blue liveried Class 20s Nos 20096 and 20107 arrive at Melton Mowbray from the Old Dalby branch working 7X09, 11.20 Old Dalby–West Ruislip S-stock move, on 22 September 2014.

During the Mid Norfolk Railway's autumn diesel gala a colourful Class 37 treble is seen passing Thuxton with BR green D6700 leading West Coast Railways No. 37706 and BR blue No. 37003 *Dereham Neatherd High School 1912 – 2012* working 1W13, the 15.12 Dereham–Wymondham Abbey service, on 22 September 2013.